Real Estate

Money and Me

Real Estate

by
Wendy Sacket and
Christine L. Hainsworth-Straus

Rourke Publications, Inc.
Vero Beach, FL 32964

Photo on page 2 by Jim Whitmer.

Produced by Salem Press, Inc.

∞ The paper used in these volumes conforms to the American National
Standard for Permanence of Paper for Printed Library Materials, Z39.48-1984.

Library of Congress Cataloging-in-Publication Data
Sacket, Wendy, 1962-
   Real Estate / by Wendy Sacket and Christine L. Hainsworth-Straus.
      p.   cm. — (Money and me)
   Includes bibliographical references and index.
   Summary: Explains the buying and selling of real estate and the role played
by real estate brokers.
   ISBN 0-86625-612-1
   1. House buying — United States — Juvenile literature. 2. Residential real
estate — United States — Purchasing — Juvenile literature. 3. Real estate
business — United States — Juvenile literature. [1. House buying. 2. Real estate
business.] I. Hainsworth-Straus, Christine L., 1962-   II. Title. III. Series.
HD255.S23   1997
333.33 — dc21   97-6818
                                                                                          CIP
                                                                                          AC

First Printing

Contents

CHAPTER 1

What Is Real Estate?

Every day, people are busy buying items they need. The biggest purchase most people ever make has to do with *real estate*. Real estate involves the ownership of real *property*. Such property includes land, buildings, and anything permanently attached to the land or buildings. The sale of property is similar to any other kind of sale. It usually just involves more money.

Buying and Selling

One day, Carrie, Marcus, and Raul were playing in Carrie's backyard. They decided to have a yard sale. First, they collected some of their old books and toys to sell to their friends. Next, they made a sign to put on the sale table. The sign listed the price of the books at seventy-five cents. The price of small toys was one dollar and the price of large toys was two dollars. The three friends set up their table on the sidewalk in front of Carrie's house.

Their friend Lily walked up to see what was on the table. She picked out a book and a large teddy bear. Lily said she would buy them if she could pay two dollars and fifty cents. Carrie, Marcus, and Raul agreed to sell the items to her. They would sell the bear and book for two dollars and fifty

Yard sales teach children about the fundamentals of buying and selling. **(Tony Cuevas)**

cents instead of the two dollars and seventy-five cents they were asking. Lily asked her friends to save her choices since she had to leave for her ballet lesson.

Fifteen minutes later, Alex walked up to the table. He looked at the toys and found a dump truck that he liked. He also saw the teddy bear that Lily wanted. Marcus told Alex that they were saving the bear for Lily. Alex said that he would pay two dollars and twenty-five cents for the bear. Carrie, Marcus, and Raul looked at each other. They wanted to sell the bear for more money, but they knew they had promised to save it for Lily. They didn't want to disappoint Alex, but they knew they had to honor their contract with Lily.

What Is a Contract?

Like at the yard sale, a real estate buyer has to reach an agreement with the current owner to own a piece of property. This agreement is called a contract. It describes the land and buildings that are being sold. It also lists all the conditions that the buyer and the seller must meet. Then the buyer and seller can exchange *consideration* (money) and transfer ownership for a piece of real estate. This transfer is confirmed by a *deed*, or written document, that proves ownership. Contracts can be oral or written. The contract is legal and must be followed if the components, or parts, of a contract are there.

A real estate contract, or *purchase agreement*, requires the following parts: competent parties, valuable consideration, offer and acceptance, and lawful object. Nearly every real estate contract must be in writing, and all parties must sign it.

MONOPOLY AND REAL ESTATE

The game of Monopoly® has elements that relate to the business of real estate. Each property on the game board can be purchased from the bank for a certain price. The buyer receives a game card that lists how much rental income can be charged to other players who land on the property. The rent increases when the property has houses or hotels on it. The back of the card lists the amount of money the bank will pay if the player has to sell the property back to the bank. There is no limit to the amount of money or property players can receive for selling or trading properties with one another. In real life, most people cannot actually afford to pay cash for real estate. With that exception, the conditions in a Monopoly game reflect common practices in the world of real estate.

Competent parties means that people are mentally competent. The parties in a real estate deal must be of legal age. This age is defined by the state in which the real estate is located. Carrie, Marcus, and Raul were competent parties at the yard sale because they owned the items they offered for sale.

Valuable consideration is anything of value given or promised — usually money. Lily promised to bring money to buy the bear and the book. Offer and acceptance requires an offer of objects and services and an acceptance of the offer. The promise to sell requires the seller to sell under those terms. Lily offered to buy the objects, and her friends accepted her offer.

A lawful object is an object to which ownership can be proved and transferred. At the yard sale, the objects were the toys and books. As owners, the three friends had the right to sell these objects. They could transfer ownership to Lily.

Being a smart shopper, Lily tried to *negotiate* a lower price. To negotiate means to arrive at a price by mutual agreement. At the yard sale, the three friends set prices they felt were fair. Lily began to negotiate by offering a price she was willing to pay. The friends accepted Lily's offer although it was less than the price they had set. Sometimes both parties are not willing to negotiate. Therefore, they do not reach an agreement.

Sometimes more than one buyer will offer to purchase the same object. Lily and Alex both wanted to buy the same teddy bear. They made separate offers at different prices. Lily made her offer first. It was accepted first, so the three friends had to honor it. Alex's offer of more money was tempting, but they already had an agreement with Lily. This situation often happens in the business world and in the world of real estate sales.

When Lily returned from her ballet lesson, she brought her money. She paid the three friends two dollars and fifty cents. Raul handed her the book, and Carrie gave her the teddy bear. The transfer of property took place under the terms of the contract, and Lily became the new owner. Both parties completed their portion of the contract.

Types of Real Estate

Real estate contracts apply to many different types of real property. Residential real estate usually refers to houses and *townhouses* that people own individually. *Condominiums* and *cooperatives* are other types of residential real estate that involve different forms of individual ownership.

Another type of real estate is commercial real estate. It includes office buildings and apartment complexes where tenants rent units. Commercial real estate also includes retail centers, or properties where there are stores and other businesses that sell merchandise and services.

A third type of real estate is industrial real estate. This type of real estate includes manufacturing plants that produce manufactured goods and warehouses that store them. Industrial real estate also includes research and development facilities where companies design, test, and produce various goods and products.

Many of the same procedures and laws apply to the sale of these three types of real estate. The examples in this book will deal primarily with residential real estate.

CHAPTER 2

How Do People Afford Real Estate?

Home Economics

Each year in the United States, millions of dollars worth of real estate is sold. The National Association of Realtors (NAR) reported that sales of previously owned homes reached 4.09 million in 1996. This amount broke the old record of 3.99 million homes set in 1978.

How do people come up with the large amounts of money needed to buy real estate? Home buyers must know about their own personal finances before they can figure out whether they can afford to purchase real estate.

Carrie, Marcus, and Raul have become good friends with their new neighbor, Alex Johnson. His

ELEMENTS IN THE HOME-BUYING PROCESS

- determining the kind of housing you need
- finding a home and rating how well it meets your housing needs
- pricing the property by comparing its features with those found in other properties with known values (recently sold or listed)
- getting a loan to finance the purchase of the property
- closing the transaction

family just bought a house in the neighborhood. The Johnsons learned about the state of their personal finances when they bought their new house.

Knowing How Much You Spend

Many people's incomes and spending habits change from month to month. Most individuals do, however, develop a spending routine. Their income equals the total money they earn or receive. Adults receive most of their earnings in the form of a paycheck. They may also receive earnings from investments. These earnings include interest paid on money in their savings accounts. It also includes dividends paid on their investments in shares of company stock or mutual funds.

After depositing their earnings in a bank account, most people spend this income on basic living expenses. These basic expenses include housing, groceries, car payments, and other necessary items. Experts say that the money a

Families who are considering the purchase of a new home need to budget wisely. (PhotoDisc, Inc.)

person spends on housing for one month should be less than half of their monthly income.

People might want to spend more than half of their monthly income on housing, but they do have other expenses. People use some of their income to pay credit card bills and bills for water, electricity, gas, telephones, and other utilities. They also use money to buy "not-so-necessary" items, including movie tickets or compact discs. Sometimes there is money left over that becomes part of their savings. People who want to buy homes in the future need to find ways to save large amounts of money.

When the Johnson family started thinking about buying a new house, they began by collecting information about their spending. They needed to find out how much of their current income they were saving. The Johnsons collected six months worth of old paycheck stubs, store receipts, credit card statements, and canceled checks. Going over these records provided a clear picture of where their money had gone.

Once they reviewed this information, Alex's parents set up a budget. This budget helped them plan how much money they could use to buy a new house. It also helped them plan where they would get this money. They knew that their monthly expenses would probably be larger at the new house. The Johnsons would need money to buy furniture, landscape the yard, pay higher utility bills, and make loan and property tax payments. They might need to spend more money on gasoline to drive to work, school, or shopping centers.

Borrowing Money

Buying a home is one of the most expensive financial goals that people work to achieve. Few people have enough cash to buy a house outright. They need to borrow money to pay for the real estate they purchase. Bankers and other lenders can

ANNUAL BUDGET FOR THE JOHNSON FAMILY

INCOME:

Dad's salary less payroll deductions	$25,200
Mom's salary less payroll deductions	24,060
Investment income (interest + dividends)	1,000
Total	**$50,260**

EXPENSES:

Living expenses:

Rent	$ 8,400
Utilities (gas, electricity, phone, water, trash)	2,000
Food and household supplies ($400/month)	4,800
Clothing and personal items	2,400
Car maintenance and gas (two cars)	2,000
Car registrations and fees	200
Medical (medicines, doctor and dentist visits)	1,500
Children (allowances, school supplies, lessons)	2,000
Gifts for family/friends	1,000
Entertainment and recreation	1,000

Debt:

Credit cards	0
Car payments	2,000

Insurance:

Car insurance	2,000
Medical and dental insurance	3,000
Charitable giving	2,000
Total expenses	**$34,300**
Income – Expenses	**$15,960**

SAVINGS:

Retirement savings (401K, other)	$ 6,260
Children's college funds	2,000
Emergencies	2,000
New house fund	5,700
Total savings for needs	**$15,960**

PROPOSED BUDGET FOR BUYING A HOUSE:

Current monthly rent	$	700
Monthly contribution to new house fund		475
Total budget for new house expenses	**$**	**1,175**
(monthly mortgage, insurance, maintenance)		

provide this money. They can tell their customers how much money they are qualified to borrow, but not how much they can *afford* to borrow. Banks and loan companies need to know how much money their customers receive, spend, and save. They also want to know about a person's credit history, or history of paying their bills. Once they know this information, banks and loan companies come up with an amount of money they are willing to risk lending. Bankers and other lenders need to be sure that the money they lend will be repaid to them.

What Is a Mortgage?

A *mortgage* is a loan that someone uses to buy a piece of property. A home mortgage allows people to buy a home when they do not have enough cash to pay the entire purchase price.

Home buyers must pay certain monthly costs connected with owning real estate. First, they must make payments on the *principal*, or face value of the home mortgage. Second, they must make payments on the *interest* connected with the mortgage. Interest is the money that lenders charge buyers to borrow the loan principal. Third, home buyers must pay real estate taxes and *assessments* on their property. Finally, home buyers must pay insurance premiums to protect the property they own from damage.

The acronym PITI stands for Principal, Interest, Taxes, and Insurance. It is derived from the following equation used to determine a buyer's housing expenses:
Housing expense = Mortgage payment (principal + interest) + property taxes + insurance

---

When the Johnsons established their home buying budget, they had to figure out how much of their earnings they could spend. They started with a mortgage payment they thought they could

MORTGAGE PAYMENT CALCULATOR
FOR 30-YEAR FIXED RATE LOAN

Loan Amount	6.5 percent	7.25 percent	8 percent
$ 1,000	6.32	6.82	7.34
2,000	12.64	13.64	14.68
3,000	18.96	20.47	22.01
4,000	25.28	27.29	29.35
5,000	31.60	34.11	36.69
6,000	37.92	40.93	44.03
7,000	44.24	47.75	51.36
8,000	**50.57**	**54.57**	58.70
9,000	56.89	61.39	**66.04**
10,000	63.21	68.22	**73.38**
20,000	126.41	**136.44**	146.75
30,000	**189.62**	204.65	220.13
40,000	252.83	272.87	293.51
50,000	316.03	341.09	366.88
60,000	379.24	409.31	440.26
70,000	442.45	477.52	513.64
80,000	505.65	545.74	587.01
90,000	568.86	613.96	660.39
100,000	**632.07**	**682.18**	**733.96**

To make a monthly payment of approximately $875 on a 30-year fixed-rate loan at interest rate of 7.25 percent:

682.18 + 136.44 + 54.47 = $873.09 monthly payment
100,000 + 20,000 + 8,000 = $128,000 loan

With an interest rate of 8 percent, you could only borrow $119,000:

733.96 + 73.38 + 66.04 = $873.38 monthly payment
100,000 + 10,000 + 9,000 = $119,000 loan ($9,000 less)

With an interest rate of 6.5 percent, you could borrow $138,000:

632.07 + 189.62 + 50.57 = $872.26
100,000 + 30,000 + 8,000 = $138,000 loan (10,000 more)

afford. The Johnson family assumed they could afford a monthly loan payment of $875.00.

Next, they needed to know the loan period, or number of years that they would be making payments on the loan. They also needed to know how much interest a bank or loan company would charge them for borrowing money. The loan's *interest rate* is expressed as a percentage. From looking in the newspaper, the Johnsons learned that the lowest interest offered on thirty-year *fixed-rate loans* was 7.25 percent. Using the mortgage payment calculator below, they could afford a $128,000 thirty-year fixed-rate loan. Their monthly mortgage payment (principal plus interest) would be $873.09.

The Johnsons decided to make a *down payment* of $32,000. Adding this down payment to the total loan of $128,000 meant that Johnsons could afford to buy a house worth $160,000.

There were other costs the Johnsons had to include in their home buying budget. They needed to have money to pay for *homeowners insurance*. The approximate monthly insurance on a house worth $160,000 is $53. Most homeowners pay for some repairs and improvements each year, such as fixing a leaky faucet or buying new garbage cans. This annual maintenance on a $160,000 house typically is equal to $1,600 — or $133 per month. Typical property taxes may be 1.5 percent of the purchase price — $2,400 per year, or $200 per month. These extra costs brought the Johnsons' total monthly housing payment to $1,259.09.

Types of Mortgages

The Johnsons weren't sure they could afford such a large monthly payment for their new house. First, they thought about choosing a home in a lower price range so they could begin with a smaller loan. That way they could save more money before buying a more expensive house.

Alex knew from reading the newspaper that his parents could choose to shop around for a different kind of loan instead. There are two basic types of loans. The Johnsons based their original budget on borrowing money through a *fixed-rate loan*, also known as a conventional loan. This mortgage loan has a fixed rate of interest during the full term of

Loan officers can help explain the advantages and disadvantages of fixed-rate and adjustable-rate mortgages to their customers. (Ben Klaffke)

the loan. These loans are attractive because their monthly payments (principal and interest) are exactly the same during the entire loan period.

There are some disadvantages to fixed-rate loans. Interest rates are usually higher for fixed-rate loans. If interest rates fall, the borrowers can't benefit from these lower rates unless they refinance their loans. Another disadvantage is that the minimum down payment on fixed-rate loans is usually fairly high. Borrowers must pay at least 10 to 20 percent of the purchase price out of their own pockets to qualify for a fixed-rate loan. In addition, interest rates on *nonconforming loans* may be higher than those on *conforming loans*. Conforming loans are less than a certain limit in each state. Nonconforming loans are also known as jumbo loans because they exceed these loan limits.

The Johnsons learned they could afford a larger loan if they looked for an *adjustable-rate mortgage* (ARM). ARMs are sometimes called variable-rate mortgages. Such mortgages have monthly payments that vary, or change, during the loan period. The loan's interest rate goes up and down. These loans are attractive because borrowers can make smaller loan payments when interest rates fall. With falling interest rates, borrowers might decide instead to make larger payments against the principal. The main disadvantage with an ARM is that borrowers must make larger loan payments when interest rates increase.

Who Makes a Real Estate Transaction Work?

Once the Johnsons knew what kind of house they wanted and how much they could afford to pay for it, they needed a real estate *agent*.

Working with Real Estate Agents

Usually when people buy real estate, they work with an agent. Agents are licensed by the state as professionals in the real estate practice. In addition to showing properties that are for sale, agents arrange the details of *escrows* or closings. They must be employed by a person or corporation that is licensed as a real estate *broker*. Agents and brokers coordinate the functions of other professionals who work on real estate transactions. These professionals include mortgage brokers, *appraisers*, building inspectors, and title officers.

The Johnsons' agent showed them many homes that were for sale. One of the homes they saw had many features the Johnsons wanted. It had three bedrooms plus a room that could be used as an office for Alex's father. Alex's mother liked its large

Real estate agents work hard to find properties that meet the needs of their clients. (PhotoDisc, Inc.)

kitchen and was happy that the house was located in a good school district. Alex and his sister Mollie liked the big backyard. Alex and Mollie had seen their parents read advertisements in the real estate section of the newspaper. They had a good idea of how much money the home they liked should cost. The Johnsons were ready to make an offer on the home. Their agent helped negotiate and write up the details of their offer.

The Johnsons had their real estate agent present an offer to the seller's broker. The written offer identified the property by its address and location.

ABBREVIATIONS USED IN REAL ESTATE ADVERTISEMENTS

A/C = air conditioning
att gar = attached garage
ba = bathroom
bdrm = bedroom
condo = condominium
DR = dining room
frplc = fireplace
LR = living room
no HOA = no homeowners' association or association fees
nu kit = new/remodeled kitchen
pvt. gar. = private garage
rec rm = recreation room
sq. ft. = square feet (for measuring interior house space)
twnhm = townhome or condominium
w/w carp = wall-to-wall carpeting

The offer also described how the Johnsons would pay for the property. The sellers had to respond to the Johnsons' offer within a certain period. The sellers could accept the terms or negotiate new terms. The offer also identified any *contingencies* connected with it. Contingencies are conditions or events that would make the buyers or sellers change their minds about completing the contract. The Johnsons also had to place a deposit (also called *earnest money*) in the hands of the broker.

Negotiating a Deal

The sellers and the Johnsons entered negotiations after the broker presented the Johnsons' offer. The two sides made a series of *counteroffers*. Counteroffers are often drawn up as amendments (changes or additions) to the original written offer. During negotiations, most agents, brokers, and lawyers encourage their clients to work together. By working together, everyone is satisfied by the agreement. Sellers want to feel that they will receive a fair price for their property.

Buyers want to feel that they have paid a fair price and are getting their money's worth.

In drawing up their offer, the Johnsons' agent discussed the important elements of a real estate purchase contract. These elements included the purchase price of the home, the down payment the Johnsons would have to make, and the financing they would need to secure. Their agent also talked about *appraisals*, inspections, and title holdings. Finally, the agent promised to advise the Johnsons about closing dates and division of *closing costs*. A closing date must be established when a contract is written. On the day of closing, when all elements of the contract are fulfilled and title to the property is being transferred, certain closing costs must be paid. Closing costs refer to various fees, including agents' fees, that must be paid before the sale of the property is final. These costs range from two to five percent of the home's purchase price and are paid in addition to the down payment.

The Johnsons and their agent came up with an amount of money they would offer to pay the sellers. When the sellers agreed to the Johnsons' offer, the Johnsons had their agent create a written contract. This contract included many of the same

When negotiating the terms of a written offer, agents often work out the details at their clients' homes. **(James L. Shaffer)**

conditions and types of information found in the Johnsons' offer.

A real estate contract is a more formal legal document than an offer. A contract lists everything on the property that is included in the sale. Any items that are not listed are not included in the sale. Sometimes sellers want to take some indoor items with them. They may want to keep their refrigerator, washer, dryer, free-standing stove, microwave oven, and chandeliers or other lighting fixtures. They may also want to take outdoor items such as swing sets, basketball hoops, and sandboxes. Such items can be excluded.

Down Payments and Financing

A down payment is the money or consideration that is deposited with a third party before a real estate transaction is closed. The Johnsons did not have an old house that they were selling. They had to use money they saved to make the down payment. They could also use money presented to them as a gift by relatives. The down payment represents the portion of the purchase price that the Johnsons did not finance through a bank or loan company.

Financing is the loan package that allows the buyer to make up the difference between their down payment and the purchase price. Home loans are usually financed for many years. To qualify for these loans, buyers must meet certain guidelines, such as having steady employment and a good credit history. Buyers usually make monthly payments on these loans or mortgages. Buyers repay a portion of the principal with each monthly mortgage payment. This process is called *amortization*. The payments also include the interest that the lender charges for the use of the money. Loan payments during the early years of a mortgage go mostly toward paying off the interest.

Mortgage brokers advise their customers about the details of the loans they offer.
(Ben Klaffke)

Working with Mortgage Brokers

Mortgage brokers are professionals who make financing available to buyers. These brokers know the various lenders and mortgage companies who offer real estate loans. Mortgage brokers handle the negotiations between buyers and mortgage lenders. The Johnsons found a loan they could afford with the help of a mortgage broker.

Sometimes people must get private mortgage insurance (PMI) to secure a loan. They need this insurance if they are making a down payment of less than 20 percent of the purchase price. Private mortgage insurance helps guarantee that the mortgage lender will not lose money if the buyers can't meet their loan payments. Once the *equity* (ownership) in the buyers' property increases to 20 percent, they don't need to carry this insurance.

Evaluating and Appraising a House

The mortgage broker who worked with the Johnsons told them that the loan company would need to know the fair market value of the house they were buying. Banks and loan companies need this information before they will give buyers a mortgage. Information about property values is gathered by people who are called appraisers. Appraisers estimate the current market value of a property. Appraisers can't have any private interest in the value of the properties they appraise.

Appraisers gather information about recent sales of similar properties. They use the selling price of one property to value other properties still on the market. They use these comparable sales ("comps")to set the house's fair market value. The appraiser's written estimates are called an *appraisal*. Appraisals confirm whether the purchase price is fair. Appraisers sometimes use a cost approach technique when a property has unusual qualities. Such qualities make it hard for appraisers to find comparable houses.

Inspecting the Property

Before they could close their real estate deal, the Johnsons had to work with a building inspector. This inspector examined the physical condition of the property the Johnsons were buying. Inspectors make sure that buildings are safe. They also look to see if the building meets guidelines established in *zoning ordinances* and *building codes*. Zoning ordinances are safety laws established by city,

Building inspectors carefully examine the physical condition of the properties they are hired to inspect. (PhotoDisc, Inc.)

county, and state government agencies. These laws allow the construction of certain types of buildings. These laws may limit the uses of buildings based on their location or zoning. Real estate contracts usually require that an inspection take place soon after the buyers and sellers reach an agreement. This inspection tells buyers and lenders whether the property is in good condition.

Buyers sometimes hire additional inspectors to look for termite damage. Some inspectors will look for structural damage to the house (including damage from earthquakes and flooding). Other inspectors will look for the presence of radon, asbestos, and other hazardous materials. If these inspectors find problems, someone must make the repairs and pay for them. The buyer and seller will negotiate to see who will do this.

The Role of a Title Officer

Before ownership of the house could be transferred to the Johnsons, they had to work with a title officer. A title officer makes a *title search* to verify who is the legal owner. The title officer searches all public records of legal ownership to determine the current ownership of a piece of property. Research done by title officers produces a complete history of a piece of property. This history tells how the property was transferred or divided over time. The result of this research is called a "chain of title."

Buyers will have to pay for title insurance once they take possession of their new property. This insurance is required and is expensive. Title insurance policies can be issued only after title is determined. This insurance protects the lender in case any prior claim to the property exists.

Owners have three basic ways of holding title to a property. Sole proprietors are owners who buy properties by themselves. Joint tenants are owners who have equal interest and rights in the property. If one joint tenant dies, the other tenant automatically becomes the sole owner. Sometimes two or more owners choose to hold title as tenants in common. These co-owners may have unequal interest in the property. Their share in the property can be sold or willed to someone other than a co-owner. Some married couples hold title as tenants in the entireties. Under this arrangement, each spouse has a complete interest in the property. Community property rules apply in certain states. These rules hold that any real estate acquired during a marriage belongs equally to both parties. As a result, both parties must agree to the sale of such property.

Other Jobs Connected to Real Estate

The Johnsons worked with many real estate professionals when they bought their new home. The house was new to them, but it was not a brand new house. There are other real estate professionals who work to build and sell new houses.

Developers and builders take the risk of adding improvements to a piece of land. They may work alone as individuals or together as companies. Such individuals and companies see a need for the building—whether it is a house, office tower, or warehouse facility. They use their money and skills to construct these buildings. The developers and builders sell the property to a buyer or lease it to tenants once the buildings are finished. Builders are usually members of local building industry associations and the National Association of Home Builders.

Developers and builders usually hire architects to design their buildings. Such individuals and firms decide what the building will look like. Architects must understand how an owner or tenant will use the building before they can complete their designs.

DONALD JOHN TRUMP

Born on June 13, 1946, in Queens, New York, Donald Trump was the son of a successful developer and manager of apartment buildings. He worked in his father's business during high school and college before graduating with a bachelor's degree from the Wharton School of Finance at the University of Pennsylvania in 1968.

Determined to make a name for himself in New York City's fast-paced business world, Trump worked on a deal in 1974 to restore and improve the old Commodore Hotel in downtown Manhattan. Trump convinced executives with the Hyatt Hotel corporation to join in the rebuilding effort. He also persuaded the city government to grant the project a huge tax break — $120 million — to help him finance the project. After Trump and his colleagues opened the new Grand Hyatt Hotel near Grand Central Station, many developers began to clean up and rebuild other properties in the area.

Famous high-rise offices, hotels, and casino buildings developed by Trump include Trump Tower on Fifth Avenue, Trump Parc, and Trump Palace in New York City, plus Trump Castle and Trump Taj Mahal in Atlantic City. Trump published his autobiography, entitled *Trump: The Art of the Deal*, in 1987. In the book, he tells of the way he used his knowledge of the financial requirements of developing real estate to persuade other people to lend him money for his projects.

In 1996, Trump completed the renovation of the old Gulf and Western building at Columbus Circle and Central Park in Manhattan. He renamed the property the Trump International Hotel and Tower.

Contractors on a building site look at blueprints to be sure they are following the design specifications made by the project's architect and engineer. (James L. Shaffer)

They also need to know the city codes that apply to the project.

Engineers work closely with architects in designing and planning buildings. Such individuals and firms look at the architect's drawings and decide how the building should be built. Engineers use their scientific knowledge to ensure that the structure of a building is safe. They make notes about the physical stresses and forces a building must survive. Engineers understand the way that building materials and land types (geologic conditions) will affect a building. They also know the restrictions that apply to the structure and surrounding property.

Once the architects and engineers have agreed on a design, they turn over the building plans to building contractors. Contractors are the people who actually construct the building based on the architect's plans and the engineer's specifications. Such individuals and firms often hire workers to help them. Some of these workers are called subcontractors. Subcontractors are experts in certain areas of building, such as plumbing or laying tiles. They hire their own workers to build certain parts of the building or install fixtures within the building.

CHAPTER 4

What Are the Rules?

Important rules apply to the sale and transfer of real estate. Agents, brokers, and other real estate professionals must obey these rules. State and local governments have agencies that control how real estate business is handled. The federal government also has agencies that oversee laws and regulations that apply to real estate.

Licensing

Each state has its own agency that sets the requirements that people must meet to be licensed agents or brokers. Most states have basic requirements that must be completed by all license holders. People who apply for a real estate license must complete a certain number of hours of classroom education. They must also pass a state examination. Brokers must complete more classroom hours and take a more difficult examination than agents do. Brokers usually cover more subject matter because they oversee more transactions. Individuals who are licensed in one of the fifty states can often practice real estate in another state with little or no additional testing. State real estate commissions operate under the rule of reciprocity. Reciprocity allows the states

to recognize and respect one another's licensing
standards.

Most states participate in one of two national
testing systems. These systems place uniform
questions on the part of the real estate examination
that applies to federal law. The sections applying
to state law vary. Individuals must learn and be
tested on this material to practice in another state
if full reciprocity is not granted between the states.

State real estate departments and commissions have the right to take away someone's real estate license. Agents and brokers can lose their licenses if they violate the Realtor's code of ethics. They can also lose their license for breaking state laws. They may also have to pay heavy fines. Real estate transactions represent one of the largest individual investments that a person will make. State commissions will punish individuals who violate the legal and ethical standards of the real estate profession.

Real Estate Credentials

The term Realtor® is a registered trademark. It identifies a real estate broker who is an active member of a real estate board connected with the National Association of Realtors (NAR). Realtors are subject to the rules set up by the NAR. They must observe the association's standards of conduct and may enjoy its benefits. Licensed brokers may join the national group, but they may choose to be members of the state or local affiliate only.

State and local boards of Realtors operate in most communities. These local boards provide the multiple listing service (MLS) of properties available for sale in the community. This computerized

---

THE CHANGING WORLD OF REAL ESTATE SALES

Internet access is changing the way real estate business is conducted. There are real estate consultants who can provide information about features of new housing developments on CD-ROM. Many real estate agents and agencies have information sites, known as home pages or Web pages, on the Internet. These sites provide some of the information that agents and brokers share with one another on computerized multiple listing services. There may even be photographic images of properties available for sale. Other companies provide online services with nationwide listings and information about home buying and home mortgage rates. Homeowners who are selling their own homes may use sites that accept text listings at no charge and can include pictures and further details about homes for an additional monthly charge.

service allows members to advertise the properties they are representing for sale. Other members who want to show these properties to their clients can contact the sales agent.

Most sales of real estate in the United States are done by two brokers who work together on one transaction. One broker represents the seller, and one represents the buyer. A single broker wants to avoid any charges of unfair representation that might arise because of a conflict of interest. These brokers must notify the buyer and the seller that they are acting as a dual representative. Having two brokers avoids problems that may occur when one party represents both the buyer and the seller in a transaction.

Loans and Government Policy

Several agencies of the federal government influence lending policies and the availability of mortgages. These agencies regulate and encourage mortgage loans. They also control interest rates and the money supply. Changes in interest rates and money supply usually happen gradually over several months or years. Even a small change can affect a person's ability to afford real estate. Low interest rates help home buyers get loans more easily. When interest rates go up, it is harder for people to get the loans they need to buy real estate. People need to consider how the federal government's actions might affect them when they decide to buy real estate.

Ginnie Mae, Fannie Mae, and Freddie Mac

Three federal agencies work with loans sold in the secondary mortgage market. These agencies buy up large blocks of mortgage loans in the form of bonds or notes. Next, they sell these bonds or notes to large investors, such as insurance companies, mutual funds, or pension funds. One agency is the

Government National Mortgage Association (GNMA), also known as "Ginnie Mae." Another is the Federal National Mortgage Association (FNMA), also known as "Fannie Mae." The third agency is the Federal Home Loan Mortgage Corporation (FHLMC), known as "Freddie Mac." These three agencies guarantee the loans they buy and resell. They guarantee that the federal government will pay back these loans if the borrowers *default*, or stop making payments.

Other Federal Agencies

The Federal Home Loan Bank (FHLB) is an agency that regulates the credit reserves and loan policies of savings and loan associations. Savings and loans have been responsible for issuing most home mortgages in the United States.

Other federal agencies are involved in insuring and guaranteeing mortgage loans. The Federal Housing Administration (FHA) was created in 1934 to insure mortgages. It later set up loan procedures that helped create the secondary mortgage market. The Veterans Administration (VA) became responsible for administering a loan-guarantee program for soldiers who fought in World War II. Its program later expanded to serve veterans of other wars and of the "peacetime" armed forces. In 1972, the Farmers Home Administration took charge of guaranteeing loans to finance home ownership on farms and in rural areas. Its program later included special loans for other people who had difficulty in qualifying for financing.

Fair Housing

U.S. law prohibits discrimination in housing based on race, ethnicity, religion, gender, national origin, disability, or family status. The Department of Housing and Urban Development (HUD) enforces the Fair Housing Act. This act prohibits

As secretary of Veterans Affairs under President Clinton, Jesse Brown oversees the loan guaranty programs that began under the Veterans Administration. (AP/Wide World Photos)

anyone from denying housing to another person. It states that no one can refuse to sell, rent, or negotiate with another person, or offer different terms and conditions based on the categories listed above. Advertisements related to housing may not contain language that excludes certain people. State and local zoning and land use ordinances can't treat any person unfairly. Anyone found guilty of threatening or interfering with people who are exercising their rights under the Fair Housing Act can be prosecuted in federal court.

Other federal laws apply to equal opportunity in housing by guaranteeing fairness in lending. These laws include the Equal Credit Opportunity Act of 1974, the Home Mortgage Disclosure Act of 1975, and the Real Estate Settlement Procedure Act of 1974 (known as RESPA).

Truth in Lending

A rule passed by Federal Reserve Board in September of 1996 requires mortgage brokers to obey the terms of the Truth in Lending Act. Mortgage brokers must tell what loan fees they charge when they issue a loan, including *origination fees*. This statement is called a truth-in-lending disclosure. Mortgage brokers must tell what fees are paid directly by borrowers. They also have to tell what fees they are charging as part of the finance charge. Brokers have to explain how these fees affect the annual percentage rates (APRs) they quote for their loans. Borrowers should ask questions when they apply for a loan. They should ask competing brokers and lenders for an estimate of the charges that will show up on the truth-in-lending disclosures.

What Are the Risks and Benefits?

Buying a home can sometimes be a very emotional experience. Buyers and sellers have to deal with different pressures. They must meet deadlines quickly. They must read and fill out plenty of paperwork. They may even regret some of the decisions they have made. Some agents and brokers tell buyers to make two lists. One list describes everything they like about the house they are buying. The other list describes everything they might want to change. These lists provide buyers with a snapshot of the home's advantages and disadvantages. The lists also encourage people to take a common-sense attitude about their decision to buy.

The Johnsons took certain risks in buying their new home. Alex's parents took on a large amount of debt. They suddenly owed more money to the bank than they had ever owed before. They could lose the house if anything happened that stopped them from making the mortgage payments. They also received benefits that helped outweigh some of these risks.

Tax Benefits

There are many tax benefits connected with owning real estate. All taxes on property are deductible as long as the property is not used for business. These taxes must be based a property's *assessed value*. The interest on a home mortgage is tax deductible up to a $1 million dollar limit as long as it is from loans secured by a person's primary or second home (including first and second mortgages, home equity loans, and refinanced mortgages). Only $100,000 in interest is deductible for all home equity loans taken out to pay off consumer debt, car loans, and school loans after October 13, 1987. There are other limits on the amount of interest that is deductible based on a person's adjusted gross income as reported on their federal income tax forms.

Loan *points*, or fees charged up front to increase a loan's effective interest rate, are deductible in the year they are paid under certain guidelines. The

Many agents encourage clients to consider all the features of the house they want to buy— features they like and those they want to change. **(James L. Shaffer)**

loan must be used to purchase or build a primary residence and must by secured by that residence. The loan's closing statement also must clearly state that these fees are points or discount points.

Some of the tax benefits are connected to other aspects of owning real estate. Prepaid property taxes that are part of the closing costs in buying a home are tax deductible. Prepaid interest on an

Mowing the lawn is one of the satisfactions—and responsibilities—that often comes with owning a home. (Jim Whitmer)

existing mortgage assumed by a new owner can be deducted from taxes as long as the new owner (buyer) pays the original owner (seller) this interest. Some moving expenses connected with buying a home are tax deductible. There may be some tax benefits connected with the profits sellers receive on the sale of their old home.

Income Tax Deductions

People who sell their homes when they are fifty-five years old or older may receive other tax benefits. If they meet these age requirements on the date of the sale of their primary home, they are allowed an income tax deduction of up to $125,000 on the profits they receive. This deduction may only be taken once. To qualify, a person must have owned and lived in the house for at least three of the five years before the date it is sold. If a person is married to someone who has already used the one-time deduction, they cannot qualify for a deduction on any homes they own with this spouse.

Feeling Satisfied

The Johnsons were very happy when they purchased their new home. Alex, Mollie, and their parents worked hard to pack up their belongings in the moving van. They were eager to move in to the new house. The entire family found new friends among the neighbors living near them at their new address.

Glossary

adjustable rate mortgage: a loan with an interest rate that is allowed to change, within certain limits, during the life of the loan.

agent: a person licensed by a state's real estate commission to handle real estate transactions. An agent must be employed by a licensed real estate broker. Buyer's agents represent the buyer; seller's agents represent the seller.

amortization: a gradual paying off of a debt. In real estate, a mortgage is amortized every month that someone makes a loan payment that covers both interest and principal.

appraisal: a written estimate of the value of a piece of property, usually made by an expert.

appraiser: a person who is experienced in evaluating properties using either the cost method or the comparable method.

assessment: the tax levied on property by a government agency to pay for certain improvements. These improvements may include new roads, sewer lines, and phone lines.

broker: a person who is licensed by a state to act for property owners in real estate transactions. These brokers must have certain years of experience in real estate, must complete a certain level of education, and must pass a state licensing examination.

building codes: the rules that control the design, construction, and use of structures.

closing costs: one-time charges, also known as settlement costs, that are paid when property passes from one owner to another. Closing costs include charges for title searches and insurance, attorney's fees, agents' fees, property surveys, mortgage application fees, and points.

condominiums: housing units in which the buyers own their apartments outright and have a share in the common areas (parking areas, land, entrance lobby) of the housing development.

cooperative: housing developments in which buyers purchase shares in the corporation that owns the building where the shareholders live. The number of shares varies according to the size of the apartment unit and its purchase price. Tenants hold a lease that gives them the right to their units.

deed: a written legal document that conveys title to real property.

default: the failure of a homeowner to make his or her monthly mortgage payments on time. Being in default can lead to foreclosure, by which a lender takes over ownership rights.

earnest money: an amount of money paid as a deposit, or binder, on a contract of sale.

equity: the interest or value that the owner has in real estate over and above the liens (legal claims, including the mortgage) against it. In the real estate world, equity refers to the difference between the market value of a home and the balance of the mortgage owed on it. Equity increases with each mortgage payment.

escrow: the money or deed placed in the keeping of a third party until terms of the escrow agreement between the other two sides have been fulfilled.

fixed-rate mortgage: a loan with an interest rate that remains the same during the life of the loan.

homeowners insurance: a written policy that pays to replace the personal belongings of homeowners. The liability portion of a policy protects against accidents that occur on the property. Flood and earthquake policies protect houses in case of natural disasters.

interest rate: the percentage of a sum of money that lenders charge for using that money.

mortgage: a written document that creates a lien or claim on real estate as security for the payment of a specified debt.

origination fees: a fee calculated as one percent of the loan amount. This fee is often considered to be a "prepaid" point. It is usually credited toward the total points charged for the loan.

points: prepaid interest that makes a loan more profitable for the lender without raising the interest rate on the mortgage.

principal: the amount of money that is borrowed for a loan. Monthly mortgage payments include a portion of the principal that must be repaid along with the interest that a lender is charging for the use of the money.

property: the rights that one person has in lands or goods to the exclusion of all others.

purchase agreement: a written agreement between seller and buyer detailing the terms under which the buyer agrees to buy real estate and the seller agrees to sell. This agreement is also known as a sales agreement or contract to purchase.

real estate: land and all attachments that are of a permanent nature.

title search: the examination of public records to determine ownership and claims affecting real property.

townhouses: houses that share a common walls and roofs. These houses are sometimes known as row houses or attached houses.

zoning ordinance: the act of a local government agency or other authority that defines how that property may be used.

Professional Organizations

Building Owners and Managers Association
(BOMA)
1201 New York Ave., N.W., Suite 300
Washington, DC 20005
(202) 289-7000

   Founded in 1908, this organization includes
owners, managers, developers, and investors
involved in the managements of commercial office
buildings. The association offers courses leading to
certification as real property administrator (RPA)
and systems maintenance administrator (SMA).

Institute of Real Estate Management (IREM)
430 N. Michigan Ave.
Chicago, IL 60611
(312) 661-1930

   This professional organization was founded in
1934 and has members who are real property
managers. It is affiliated with the National
Association of Realtors. IREM offers management
courses to individuals seeking certification as
certified property managers (CPM) and accredited
resident managers (ARM). Management firms can
receive designation as accredited management
organizations (AMO).

National Association of Black Real Estate
Professionals (NABREP)
P. O. Box 21421
Alexandria, VA 22320
(703) 683-1644

   This association was founded in 1984 to offer
career development and networking opportunities
for African Americans involved in real estate
design, development, engineering, management,
law, and investment.

National Association of Industrial and Office Parks (NAIOP)
1215 Jefferson Davis Highway, Suite 100
Arlington, VA 22202
(703) 979-3400

Founded in 1967, this professional organization includes members who are developers of commercial real estate properties. Other professionals interested in commercial and industrial real estate can join as associate members. The association offers workshops and seminars and maintains a resource library for use by its members and the general public.

National Association of Real Estate Brokers (NAREB)
1629 K St., N.W., No. 2, Suite 605
Washington, DC 20006
(202) 785-4477

This association was founded in 1947 to promote professional conduct and standards among black real estate brokers. The organization later opened its membership to all real estate brokers. NAREB adopted the term "Realtist" as the exclusive professional designation for its members. Like the NAR, this national association also has local boards and is represented in most major American cities.

National Association of Realtors (NAR)
430 N. Michigan Ave.
Chicago, IL 60611-4087
(312) 329-8200

This trade organization includes agents and brokers who are active in residential, commercial, and industrial real estate. Founded in 1908, the NAR is a federation of fifty state associations and more than 1,800 local real estate boards whose members are qualified to use the professional designation Realtor® or Realtor®-Associate. The association encourages its members to participate

in continuing education so that they are familiar with current practices and legal requirements in the real estate field.

Society of Industrial and Office Realtors (SIOR)
777 14th St., N.W., Suite 400
Washington, DC 20005
(202) 737-1150

Founded in 1941, this professional organization has members who work as agents and brokers in industrial and commercial real estate. The group sponsors educational courses and seminars that must be completed by prospective members, who must also complete a certain number of real estate transactions in order to be considered for membership.

Index